HOME SWEET HOME
Around the House
in the 1800s

DAILY LIFE IN AMERICA IN THE 1800s

Bleeding, Blistering, and Purging: Health and Medicine in the 1800s

Buggies, Bicycles, and Iron Horses: Transportation in the 1800s

Cornmeal and Cider: Food and Drink in the 1800s

America at War: Military Conflicts at Home and Abroad in the 1800s

From the Parlor to the Altar: Romance and Marriage in the 1800s

Guardians of the Home: Women's Lives in the 1800s

Home Sweet Home: Around the House in the 1800s

Jump Ropes, Jacks, and Endless Chores: Children's Lives in the 1800s

Reviving the Spirit, Reforming Society: Religion in the 1800s

Outlaws and Lawmen: Crime and Punishment in the 1800s

Passing the Time: Entertainment in the 1800s

Rooting for the Home Team: Sports in the 1800s

Scandals and Glory: Politics in the 1800s

The Sweat of Their Brow: Occupations in the 1800s

Saloons, Shootouts, and Spurs: The Wild West In the 1800s

HOME SWEET HOME
Around the House in the 1800s

by
Zachary Chastain

Mason Crest Publishers

Copyright © 2011 by Mason Crest Publishers. All rights reserved. No part of this publication may be reproduced or transmitted in any form or by any means, electronic or mechanical, including photocopying, recording, taping, or any information storage and retrieval system, without permission from the publisher.

MASON CREST PUBLISHERS INC.
370 Reed Road
Broomall, Pennsylvania 19008
(866)MCP-BOOK (toll free)
www.masoncrest.com

First Printing
9 8 7 6 5 4 3 2 1

Library of Congress Cataloging-in-Publication Data

Chastain, Zachary.
  Home sweet home : around the house in the 1800s / by Zachary Chastain.
      p. cm. — (Daily life in America in the 1800s)
  Includes bibliographical references and index.
  ISBN 978-1-4222-1781-8 (hardcover)   ISBN (series) 978-1-4222-1774-0
  ISBN 978-1-4222-1854-9 (pbk.)   ISBN (pbk. series) 978-1-4222-1847-1
  1. Dwellings—United States—History—19th century—Juvenile literature. 2. Home—United States—History—19th century—Juvenile literature. 3. Home economics—United States—History—19th century—Juvenile literature. 4. United States—Social life and customs—19th century—Juvenile literature. I. Title.
  GT207.C47 2011
  392.3'609730909034—dc22
                                            2010019182

Produced by Harding House Publishing Service, Inc.
www.hardinghousepages.com
Interior Design by MK Bassett-Harvey.
Cover design by Torque Advertising + Design.
Printed in USA by Bang Printing.

Contents

Introduction 6
Tmeline 8
Part I: What Makes a House a Home? 13
Part II: Cooking, Cleaning, and Keeping House 33
Part III: The Victorian House 47
Think About It 60
Words Used in This Book 61
Find Out More 62
Index 63
Picture Credits 64
About the Author and the Consultant 64

Introduction

History can too often seem a parade of distant figures whose lives have no connection to our own. It need not be this way, for if we explore the history of the games people play, the food they eat, the ways they transport themselves, how they worship and go to war—activities common to all generations—we close the gap between past and present. Since the 1960s, historians have learned vast amounts about daily life in earlier periods. This superb series brings us the fruits of that research, thereby making meaningful the lives of those who have gone before.

The authors' vivid, fascinating descriptions invite young readers to journey into a past that is simultaneously strange and familiar. The 1800s were different, but, because they experienced the beginnings of the same baffling modernity were are still dealing with today, they are also similar. This was the moment when millennia of agrarian existence gave way to a new urban, industrial era. Many of the things we take for granted, such as speed of transportation and communication, bewildered those who were the first to behold the steam train and the telegraph. Young readers will be interested to learn that growing up then was no less confusing and difficult then than it is now, that people were no more in agreement on matters of religion, marriage, and family then than they are now.

We are still working through the problems of modernity, such as environmental degradation, that people in the nineteenth century experienced for the first time. Because they met the challenges with admirable ingenuity, we can learn much from them. They left behind a treasure trove of alternative living arrangements, cultures, entertainments, technologies, even diets that are even more relevant today. Students cannot help but be intrigued, not just by the technological ingenuity of those times, but by the courage of people who forged new frontiers, experimented with ideas and social arrangements. They will be surprised by the degree to which young people were engaged in the great events of the time, and how women joined men in the great adventures of the day.

When history is viewed, as it is here, from the bottom up, it becomes clear just how much modern America owes to the genius of ordinary people, to the labor of slaves and immigrants, to women as well as men, to both young people and adults. Focused on home and family life, books in this series provide insight into how much of history is made within the intimate spaces of private life rather than in the remote precincts of public power. The 1800s were the era of the self-made man and women, but also of the self-made communities. The past offers us a plethora of heroes and heroines together with examples of extraordinary collective action from the Underground Railway to the creation of the American trade union movement. There is scarcely an immigrant or ethic organization in America today that does not trace its origins to the nineteenth century.

This series is exceptionally well illustrated. Students will be fascinated by the images of both rural and urban life; and they will be able to find people their own age in these marvelous depictions of play as well as work. History is best when it engages our imagination, draws us out of our own time into another era, allowing us to return to the present with new perspectives on ourselves. My first engagement with the history of daily life came in sixth grade when my teacher, Mrs. Polster, had us do special projects on the history of the nearby Erie Canal. For the first time, history became real to me. It has remained my passion and my compass ever since.

The value of this series is that it opens up a dialogue with a past that is by no means dead and gone but lives on in every dimension of our daily lives. When history texts focus exclusively on political events, they invariably produce a sense of distance. This series creates the opposite effect by encouraging students to see themselves in the flow of history. In revealing the degree to which people in the past made their own history, students are encouraged to imagine themselves as being history-makers in their own right. The realization that history is not something apart from ourselves, a parade that passes us by, but rather an ongoing pageant in which we are all participants, is both exhilarating and liberating, one that connects our present not just with the past but also to a future we are responsible for shaping.

—Dr. John Gillis, Rutgers University Professor of History Emeritus

1800
1800 The Library of Congress is established.

1801
1801 Thomas Jefferson is elected as the third President of the United States.

1803

1803 Louisiana Purchase—The United States purchases land from France and begins westward exploration.

1804
1804 Journey of Lewis and Clark—Lewis and Clark lead a team of explorers westward to the Columbia River in Oregon.

Time Line

1825
1825 The Erie Canal is completed—This allows direct transportation between the Great Lakes and the Atlantic Ocean.

1832
1832 First building built using balloon construction: a warehouse in Chicago, built by George Washington Snow.

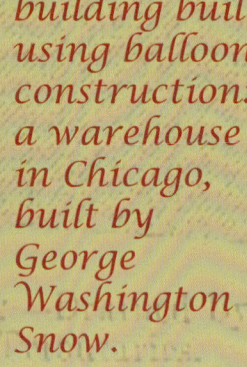

1834
1834 Oberlin Stove is invented by Philo Stewart. A compact, wood-burning, cast-iron stove that would sell some 90,000 units in the next 30 years.

1838
1838 Trail of Tears—General Winfield Scott and 7,000 troops force Cherokees to walk from Georgia to a reservation set up for them in Oklahoma (nearly 1,000 miles). Around 4,000 Native Americans die during the journey.

1806

1806 William Colgate starts a candle and soap making company in New York City—by 1900, the company will be making over 3,000 different household products.

1812

1812 War of 1812—Fought between the United States and the United Kingdom.

1820

1820 Missouri Compromise—Agreement passes between pro-slavery and abolitionist groups, stating that all the Louisiana Purchase territory north of the southern boundary of Missouri (except for Missouri) will be free states, and the territory south of that line will be slave.

1823

1823 Monroe Doctrine—States that any efforts made by Europe to colonize or interfere with land owned by the United States will be viewed as aggression and require military intervention.

1840

1840 Lowell Mill Factories in Lowell, Massachusetts, employs around 8,000 textile workers, mostly women between the ages of 16 and 35.

1843

1843 A clothes washer with wringer rolls invented by John E. Turnbull. This is the first step in a series of inventions that would lead to the modern washing machine.

1844

1844 First public telegraph line in the world is opened—between Baltimore and Washington.

1848

1848 Seneca Falls Convention—Feminist convention held for women's suffrage and equal legal rights.

1848(-58) California Gold Rush—Over 300,000 people flock to California in search of gold.

1854

1854 Kansas-Nebraska Act—States that each new state entering the country will decide for themselves whether or not to allow slavery. This goes directly against the terms agreed upon in the Missouri Compromise of 1820.

1861

1861(-65) Civil War—Fought between the Union and Confederate states.

1862

1862 Emancipation Proclamation—Lincoln states that all slaves in Union states are to be freed.

1862 Homestead Act passed, promising 160 acres of free land to any U.S. citizen. To keep their land, settlers had to build homes and "improve" upon the land.

1865

1865 Thirteenth Amendment to the United States Constitution—Officially abolishes slavery across the country.

1865 President Abraham Lincoln is assassinated on April 15.

1877

1877 Great Railroad Strike—Often considered the country's first nationwide labor strike.

1878

1878 Thomas Edison patents the phonograph on February 19.

1878 Thomas Edison invents the light bulb on October 22.

1886

1886 The Statue of Liberty is dedicated on October 28.

1890

1890 Wounded Knee Massacre—Last battle in the American Indian Wars.

1890 232,000 pianos manufactured in one year, marking a huge increase in pianos made for the home parlor.

1867

1867 United States purchases Alaska from Russia.

1867 The refrigerated railroad car is patented by J.B. Sutherland, which opens up new horizons for food and drink in homes across America.

1869

1869 Transcontinental Railroad completed on May 10.

1869 "The American Woman's Home" is published by sisters Catherine Beecher and Harriet Beecher Stowe—the book's goal is to return dignity to domestic work.

1870

1870 Fifteenth Amendment to the United States Constitution—Prohibits any citizen from being denied to vote based on their "race, color, or previous condition of servitude."

1870 Christmas is declared a national holiday.

1876

1876 Alexander Graham Bell invents the telephone.

1892

1892 Ellis Island is opened to receive immigrants coming into New York.

1896

1896 Plessy vs. Ferguson—Supreme Court case that rules that racial segregation is legal as long as accommodations are kept equal.

1896 Henry Ford builds his first combustion-powered vehicle, which he names the Ford Quadricycle.

1898

1898 The Spanish-American War—The United States gains control of Cuba, Puerto Rico, and the Philippines.

1899

1899 The Bayer company starts production of Aspirin, a first step as patent medicines improve in quality over the next century.

Part I
What Makes a House a Home?

How exactly do we define what makes a house a home? Four walls, some doors and maybe some windows, a roof over head—is that a home? Is a tent made of cured buffalo hide a home? What about a rented room with only a curtain separating your family from the other family sleeping only a few feet away—can we call that a home?

At some point in the 1800s, Americans of all kinds called each one of these living arrangements "home." Americans were in transition in the 1800s. They were moving from one way of life to another, and as they changed, so did their houses and their ideas of home.

Part I: What Makes a House a Home? 15

For one thing, the purpose of a house changed a lot between the years 1800 and 1900. In 1800, most houses were the center of production as well as family life. The purpose of a farmhouse or even a townhouse was to produce goods that sustained life. Farmhouses produced crops and other food products such as cheese and bread. In townhouses, families often lived above a store or a shop for a blacksmith, tanner, or cobbler, and they might produce in their living apartments shirts and socks, or jarred fruits and vegetables for the winter. Most activity in the house was focused primarily on supporting life. People made what they needed to survive in or near their homes.

But through the course of the 1800s, this began to change. As the Industrial Revolution took hold in America, for the first time there were more jobs outside of the house than in it. Men and women alike took to the cities looking for a job, a way to make more money and improve their way of life. The financial or economic use of the house no longer existed. The house was now a place where goods and services were consumed, not created.

At the beginning of the 1800s, the home was the place where the production of food and clothing took place. This re-creation of a nineteenth-century home in the Appalachian Mountains shows a woman spinning yarn.

By the end of the 1800s, the home had become a place where goods were consumed, especially for the wealthy, and houses started filling up with THINGS.

The Household Players: Men, Women, Children, Servants

The role of men and women in the house changed a lot in those years. When the house was the center of production, women had been partners in providing life to the family. On the frontier, where life continued to be centered around the house and not around a workplace outside the house, women continued to be partners in production.

Although this partnership was by no means perfect or without flaws, it was generally accepted that a family needed both a man and a woman to provide for all the needs of the household. The "Little House" books, written by Mary Ingalls Wilder in the 1900s, were based on her real-life experiences with her family on the American frontier in the 1800s. They show us how important both "Ma" and "Pa" are to the household. Both are constantly at work—Pa doing his chores, Ma sewing, cooking, cleaning, washing, and all the while, educating her children.

During much of the nineteenth century, both men and women helped with farm work.

EYEWITNESS ACCOUNT

Ellen Bromley tells of growing up in Illinois in the mid-1800s, revealing a world where women worked hard, cooking, planting trees—and where women also got lonely.

We lived near Warner's while we were farming. We were four miles from James Glenn's. . . . Mother said the Glenns were so hospitable. Mother was very lonesome and homesick on the farm and Mrs. Glenn had her come over and stay a week with them just to make her contented. Mrs. Glenn doctored the neighbor women and was always helpful. She would keep her Bible in the kitchen and read it while making her biscuit. One time someone came along and asked, "Why are you planting apple trees when you never will live to eat from them?" She answered, "I reckon if I don't some one else will." I guess she did live to eat apples from those trees herself.

Part I: What Makes a House a Home?

This painting shows a young family that has just moved into a new home during the nineteenth-century. It will be the wife's job now to be a "homemaker," while the husband's job will be to earn the money she needs to make their home.

Things changed for women when men started leaving the house to work, and bringing home the goods a house needed. No longer were women partners in production. No longer was the house a place of production. The house was now a retreat, a center for leisure and comfort, a comfortable place to come home to after work was completed. Women became the keepers of this place and this idea. Increasingly, women were encouraged to make themselves and their houses a "protected" place, away from the dirt and grime of the industrial, working world. The house became a place to renew one's spirit and one's morals, to learn to appreciate culture and beauty; and the woman was responsible for carrying out this effect.

A whole genre of "advice literature" sprang up in women's magazines in the late 1800s, coaching women on how to be perfect wives and mothers. An example from one advice book, called *Hill's Manual of Social and Business Forms*, reads like this:

> Whatever have been the cares of the day, greet your husband with a smile when he returns. Make your personal appearance just as beautiful as possible. Let him enter rooms so attractive and sunny that all the recollections of his home, when away from the same, shall attract him back.

Another advice magazine, called *The Household*, said it was the wife's responsibility to provide her husband " a happy home . . . the single spot of rest which a man has upon this earth for the cultivation of his noblest sensibilities."

Children

How adults viewed children changed in the 1800s. At the beginning of the century, children were more likely to be seen as miniature adults. Farm families valued children for the work they could do, and big families were considered a blessing. Because they were expected to work alongside their parents, both in and outside the house, children were given more "adult" privileges in rural and working class families. This continued to be true throughout the 1800s in both rural and poor urban houses. Wherever children were

In upper-class homes in the late 1800s, children were expected to live their lives separated from the adults in their families. They spent their time in different parts of the house, supervised by servants.

Mothers in the middle and upper classes of the later nineteenth century were responsible for teaching their children manners (such as the proper way to drink tea, as shown here) and morals.

expected to work, they were generally also expected to reach adulthood more quickly.

In the late 1800s, however, things changed as the middle class grew in America. Servants in the home and advances in technology made housework unnecessary for middle-class children. Moral and cultural upbringing was almost entirely the responsibility of the mother.

Servants

In the more rural, pre-industrial society of the early 1800s, servants were often unpaid young relatives or neighbors of the wife or head woman in a household. They helped the woman of the house with her many tasks and in exchange they learned skills from her, skills such as weaving, spinning, cooking, and cleaning.

Then two things happened. First, the Industrial Revolution attracted many working-class women away from home and into factory positions. And second, the changing idea of home required that a woman take over the cultural and spiritual leadership of a household as her fulltime job—and hire Irish or black servants to do the other jobs of the house. What was once more

Servants who cared for young children allowed upper-class mothers time and energy to focus on morals, religion, and manners.

The nursemaids and nannies who took care of nineteenth-century children were often black women or Irish immigrants.

Home Sweet Home: Around the House in the 1800s

of a "team" mentality of women working alongside one another became an employer-employee relationship. Servants of this second type were less likely to be seen as part of an "extended family." Although they often slept in the house where they worked, they rarely ate at the same table with the family. They were hired to do specific tasks that the lady of the house didn't want to do. They did not share the same work.

Hired servants in middle- and upper-class households in the later 1800s allowed "ladies" time to focus their energy on domesticity, piety, purity, and submissiveness (four traits of the "true woman" in the late nineteenth century).

Wealthy women in the 1800s were allowed lives of leisure because servants took care of daily household chores such as preparing and serving meals, housecleaning, and laundry.

What Did Houses Look Like?

In the 1800s, European houses were generally made from brick or stone, as forests were less abundant there. But America had vast stretches of untouched forests and a thriving iron industry for making cheap iron nails. These two resources combined—iron nails and cheap wood—led to the construction of a new type of home in America called "the balloon frame." The term was originally used in mockery, as many skeptics thought the new homes would blow away like a balloon at the first strong gust of wind.

Balloon frame homes were made from many strips of wood, much like the two-by-four boards of today. Also called "light frame" construction, the method looked like building a basket from wood, and then attaching coverings to the inside and outside. Instead of hiring expensive carpenters and masons to build their homes, many Americans hired a few friends, or they built their homes entirely on their own. The new method used lots of wood and lots of

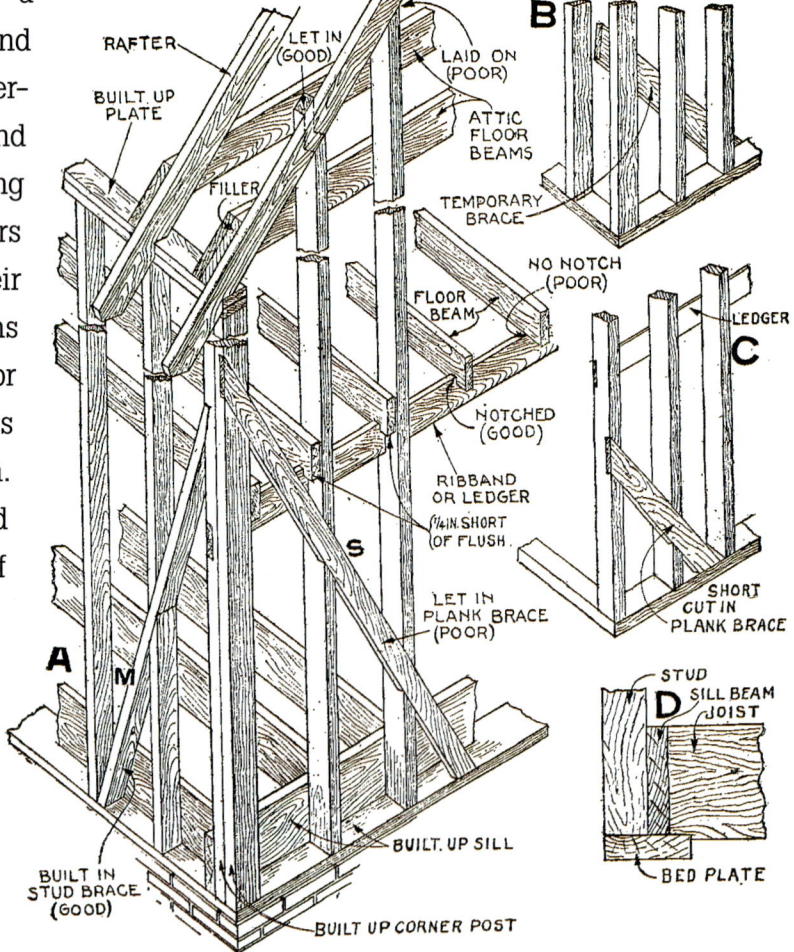

Balloon frames like this were cheap and easy to build.

26   Home Sweet Home: *Around the House in the 1800s*

nails, but it didn't take much professional knowledge, which meant it was cheap.

And it was fast too: hundreds of homes sprung up in new communities, usually made from whatever wood was available in that region. The balloon frame was stronger than it looked. It held up, and its popularity grew, especially on the frontier where people had little money but lots of ambition. Today many homes in the Midwest (the frontier of the 1800s) still have homes built by balloon-frame construction.

At first, people thought balloon-frame houses would not last—but more than a hundred years later, houses like this one are still standing.

Regional Differences

Every house was different. Southern plantation houses built at the beginning of the century were far more elaborate than the longhouses built by Native Americans in the Northeast. The longhouse was like a long tunnel in which many fires were kept and multiple families lived. Meanwhile, the slaves who lived on Southern plantations generally lived in one-room houses separate from their master's home. The slaves' houses were usually out of sight from the main house, and were like a small village with pigs or chickens roaming around and a small garden.

In the Northeast and South, middle- and lower-class families were likely to live in simple "foursquare" homes—four rooms around a single staircase that led upstairs to bedrooms and an attic above that. They usually had a cellar near the kitchen, where many foods were kept.

At the beginning of the 1800s, the houses of wealthy plantation owners in the South were large and luxurious. After the Civil War, however, many Southerners no longer had the wealth to maintain their huge homes.

Meanwhile, slaves lived in very different conditions in small houses behind the "big house."

This nineteenth-century painting portrays the private lives of blacks, hidden behind the more luxurious white-people's world. The white "mistress" is shown here peeking into the rich culture that lies behind her home.

In the Northeastern Native tribes, many families would make their homes within a longhouse like this, sleeping in the beds along the side of the walls and cooking their meals at a fire in the center. Although there was a hole in the roof, the air inside would be smoky from the fire.

EXTRA! EXTRA!

Kimball, Nebraska Daily News
August 1887

We hear tell that sod houses can be comfortable. But the popularity of this little ditty being sung tells us another story!

Soon we landed in Nebraska where they had much land to spare,

But most ever since we've been here, we've been mad enough to swear,

First we built for us a sod house and we tried to raise some trees,

But the land was full of Coyotes and our sod house full of fleas.

The family shown here with their sod house would have had to put up with dirt and insects falling on their faces while they slept and muddy floors when the weather was rainy. The house would have kept cool in summer and warm during the winter, but the interior would have been cramped and musty.

Frontier Homes

Life was different for settlers moving West than it was for people living in the more established East during the same period. On the frontier, sod houses (or "soddies"), log cabins, and shanties were the three houses of choice for pioneers. Soddies were made from thick slabs of thickly-rooted prairie grass called sod. They were not ideal homes by any stretch of the imagination. Because they were essentially made of dirt, many bugs, rodents, and other pests dropped into the house. After a hard rain, water leaking through the roof could turn the dirt floor of a sod home into a muddy mess. Some pioneers added boards and metal sheets to their sod homes in an attempt to keep water out and present a more "civilized" appearance. But most of these homes were eventually abandoned.

EYEWITNESS ACCOUNT

A woman named Mattie Oblinger wrote to a friend about her experience living in a Nebraska sod house in the late 1800s:

At Home in our own house, and a sod at that! . . . We moved in to our house last Wednesday (Uriah's birthday). I suppose you would like to see us in our sod house. It is not quite so convenient as a nice frame, but I would as soon live in it as the cabins I have lived in. And then we are at home which makes it more comfortable. I ripped our Wagon sheet in two [in order to] have it around two sides. . . . The only objection I have we have no floor yet. [It] will be better this fall.

The log cabin was by far the most popular on the frontier. It kept out wind and rain better than sod, and it lasted longer too. Log cabins were caked with mud, leaf, and twig mixtures to keep drafts from blowing through spaces in the logs, a process called "chinking." Both log cabins and sod houses were equipped with a chimney pipe or gap in the roof to allow for a fireplace or stove. Log cabins often had stone fireplaces built into them, or sometimes a chimney made from sticks and mud.

The shanty was the result of the Homestead Act passed by the U.S. Congress in the late 1800s. The act encouraged Americans to settle the West quickly by promising free land. Like the log cabin and sod house, the shanty was a quick way to build a home and lay claim to a plot of land. The Homestead Act required settlers to "prove up"—meaning they had to prove they were living permanently on the land. This meant they had to have a house of a certain size built by the time the government inspector came around. Shanties were built directly into the ground, with a dirt floor and no foundation. They consisted of a few boards nailed together and stuck into the ground, usually covered with tar paper to keep out wind and water. The shanties were less comfortable than log cabins, but about as comfortable as sod houses, and more portable than both. If an inspector came to look at a large plot of land claimed by one family, the shanty could be quickly moved from spot to spot. Americans were creative when it came to claiming their new land!

A log cabin's interior shows how simple these homes were. There was very little privacy for family members!

Part II
Cooking, Cleaning, and Keeping House

Household Chores

When you think of chores today you probably think of taking out the trash, mowing the lawn, or doing the dishes. Other chores like cooking and cleaning are made easier by technology, and almost nothing around the house requires really demanding, physical labor.

But this was not the case for most people in the 1800s. Keeping a living space sanitary, let alone beautiful and inviting, was a huge task. The large part of their housework was focused not on making it presentable for guests, but simply on keeping everyone in it healthy, warm, and well fed. Keeping house was a mater of survival!

Cooking

Consider cooking for a moment. Today, "processed" foods provide easy meals for us all. They come in plastic, cans, and boxes, and often the only tools required for preparation are a bowl or a microwave. But until factory foods came along in the late 1800s, most people spent a lot of time and energy making meals. Food usually came from nearby, either from a family's own farm or from somewhere else in the region. If you wanted chicken, you had to kill it and pluck its feathers. Fish had to have their scales removed, corn had to be shucked, coffee beans had to be roasted. So much of the preparation we take for granted today didn't exist in those days.

Many families, even those who lived in town, kept hens and dairy cows for a fresh supply of eggs, cream, milk, and churned butter. Those families in the middle and upper classes who could afford to hire servants did so; there was a lot of work to be done! Middle-class homes hired a few servants to help the housewife. Upper-class homes could afford to hire servants for individual tasks—a cook, a waitress, a laundress, a cleaning woman, a chore man. But most homes had to make due with a housewife and her daughters.

Preparing meals was a lot more work during the 1800s than it is now, as these workers at the Connor Prairie Living History Museum demonstrate. In all but the wealthiest families, all the females were expected to be responsible for cooking and cleaning, even the young ones!

Storing Food

Every home needed a place to keep cold their perishable foods, such as meat, fish, cheeses, and milk. Some wealthy estates in the North and South, where they most attempted to imitate the architecture of Europe, had a separate building called a "larder" or "buttery" for keeping such foods cold. In the South, many of the big plantation houses had a "cook house" in a separate building from the main house. This kept the smells and heat from the cooking separate from the family's living quarters.

Most nineteenth-century houses, however, had kitchens and pantries inside the main house. Pantries are special rooms for storing food. These rooms and the kitchens were usually built on the north or east sides of a house, or

Some wealthier families built ice houses like this in the 1800s. During the winter, the family would pack them with ice from a river or a lake, and the ice would last till the next year, providing a place to keep food cool.

This smokehouse was built on a Southern plantation for smoking hams, which allowed meat to stay good longer, even in hot weather.

sometimes below ground in the basement, where they would receive the least sunlight and remain as cool as possible. Families who couldn't afford larders used the darkness of basement cellars to store food. Ice harvesting became popular in the 1800s and many people bought chunks of ice and packed it around their food in the cellar.

In frontier homes, the cooking was usually done in the same room where everything else went on in the home. Settlers often buried food to keep it cold, or they stuck it in a bucket in a cold stream.

Native Americans, on the other hand, were less likely to keep any foods at all that needed cold storage. Many tribes were migratory, meaning their movement followed the movement of animal herds, so meat was always fresh. In fact, most of the food Americans—whites, blacks, and Natives—ate in the 1800s was fresh food. Salting and pickling were the only common ways to make foods last longer.

Part II: Cooking, Cleaning, and Keeping House

Getting Water

Water was always an issue for people in the 1800s, both rich and poor, Northeastern, Southern, or Western. Indoor plumbing didn't exist in most homes until the twentieth century. As an exception, some wealthy homes (especially in cities) had piped water by the late 1800s, which allowed servants to pump water from inside the house. But the majority of homes lacked an indoor water source. Most families got their water from a hydrant, pump, well, or stream located somewhere near their house. Cooking, cleaning, and washing required large amounts of water, just as they do today, and so frequent trips to the water source were necessary.

Fetching water was a tiring chore. Imagine carrying buckets of water from a pump or well eight to ten times every day—that's hundreds of gallons of water to carry over many miles of walking, just to keep water in the house! And it was usually the young girls in the house who did it.

Families thought they were lucky if they had a pump like this in their backyard, where they could get water for use inside the house.

38   *Home Sweet Home:* Around the House in the 1800s

Part II: Cooking, Cleaning, and Keeping House

Remember Jack and Jill who went up the hill to fetch a pail of water? Their chore was a common one for many children during the 1800s, especially girls.

The Stove

At the heart of every kitchen was the stove, which was a relatively recent invention. Before the stove, there was the fireplace. Fireplaces evolved into what almost looked like a stove—a partially covered pit that could be tended and used to cook. Many frontier homes of the 1800s had fireplaces of this kind in their homes. But uncovered fireplaces had many flaws: they were dirty, inefficient, and required huge amounts of wood to keep them burning all day.

The earliest "stoves" were merely enclosed fireplaces.

As inventors and entrepreneurs continued to improve the stove, they focused on making stoves better for cooking. In the early 1800s, many stoves were designed to cook by hanging pots and pans over them. By hanging a pot higher or lower over the stove, a person could roughly control the temperature. There were many, many

Frontier families and Native Americans often cooked over an outdoor open fire.

varieties to choose from. But it wasn't until the Franklin stove of the 1820s and the Oberlin stove of the 1830s that the stove became commonplace in the American home. The Oberlin stove, for example, was a huge success because it was small enough for any home and was outfitted for cooking; 90,000 Oberlin stoves were sold between 1834 and 1864. By the time of the Civil War, it was common for multiple rooms in a middle or upper class American home to have a stove. Northerners especially valued them.

The kitchen stove was the heart of a house—but keeping a stove burning was hard work. It had to be tended all day to keep the coals burning, which took up a lot of a person's time. Huge amounts of coal or wood were burned every day cooking meals and keeping warm. A typical stove had openings called "dampers" that had to be adjusted to let more or less air into the stove throughout the day. Stoves also needed to be rubbed down with a thick black wax to keep away rust and tarnish. Every morning, the ashes from the previous day had to be scraped out and replaced with fresh fuel.

Stoves were more efficient than fireplaces and used less wood, but they weren't necessarily cleaner. Smoke from stoves collected as soot on curtains, floors, and furniture. Eventually, "flues" were invented to channel smoke from stoves into pipes and out of chimneys, but until then, soot had to be cleaned constantly.

Metal stoves like this provided both heat and a cooking surface. But you couldn't turn them on simply by pressing a button or turning a knob! They took constant care and attention.

INCREDIBLE INDIVIDUAL
Catharine Beecher

Catharine Beecher had many ideas on how to make the home more efficient. In her book The American Woman's Home (which she wrote with her more famous sister, Harriet Beecher Stowe, the author of Uncle Tom's Cabin) she imagined a house more convenient for women. In the book, which is filled with drawings and floor plans for her ideal home, she envisioned how the many chores and hard work that an ordinary house required could be made easier. As it turned out, many of Beecher's imaginings would become realities in the houses of the late 1800s and early 1900s. For example, her ideal kitchen had shelves built into walls for storage, lots of work space for preparing food, and dedicated storage spaces for special foods that needed to be kept cold, dry, or moist—all realities in the modern home.

But perhaps her best idea was for heating a house. She drew pictures of a furnace that would be placed in the basement of a three-floor home. Pipes and heating ducts would extend throughout the house, making it possible to heat an entire home from one stove. Best of all, there were no open fireplaces in the system. Fresh air was brought in through one set of ducts, and smoky air was taken out of the house through another set. By the late 1800s, gas-powered stoves and furnaces were being built and installed in the homes of the wealthy, and by the early 1900s, a "centrally-heated" home was the standard for most middle-class people.

At the head of this chapter is a sketch of a house contrived for the express purpose of enabling every member of a family to labor with the hands for the common good, and by modes at once healthful, economical, and tasteful. Of course, much of the instruction conveyed in the following pages is chiefly applicable to the wants and habits of those living either in the country or in such suburban vicinities as give space of ground for healthful outdoor occupation in the family service.

So far as circumstances can be made to yield the opportunity, it will be assumed that the family state demands some outdoor labor for all. The cultivation of flowers to ornament the table and house, of fruits and vegetables for food, of silk and cotton for clothing, and the care of horse, cow, and dairy, can be so divided that each and all of the family, some part of the day, can take exercise in the pure air, under the magnetic and healthful rays of the sun. Railroads, enabling men toiling in cities to rear families in the country, are on this account a special blessing.

Laundry

Most women considered laundry to be the most back-breaking task around the house. By the end of the 1800s, a few labor-saving inventions made laundry a bit easier, but they were nothing like the electric washing machines of today.

Far from being as simple as putting laundry in a basket, doing laundry in the 1800s could be an all-day affair! Typically, whoever was doing the laundry (the housewife or a servant) soaked the dirty laundry in tubs of warm water overnight. The next morning, she scrubbed the laundry on a rough washboard and rubbed soap into it. There were no rubber gloves, and the soap was made from lye, which irritated here skin. She then dropped the clothes into a large vat of boiling water, and stirred them constantly with a long pole. With this done, she lifted the clothes out with a wash stick and rinsed them twice, once in plain water and, if the household could get it, once in a chemical called "bluing." (Bluing is a kind of bleach that makes white laundry appear whiter, and is still used in some forms today.) Finally, the clothes were wrung out and hung to dry outdoors on clotheslines. After drying, they were pressed with heavy flatirons and collars were stiffened with starch.

Depending on the size of a family, laundry could be an enormous task. By the late 1800s, some wealthy families owned "high-tech" zinc washboards, and many families bought the "wringer" or "mangler" that was invented to make squeezing water out of clothing easier.

An African American servant and her little girl do the laundry in a pot of boiling water over a fire. It was hot, exhausting work.

EYEWITNESS ACCOUNT

In 1879, Mrs. Julia McNair Wright wrote a book called *The Complete Home: An Encyclopedia of Domestic Life & Affairs*, which gives the following advice to women:

Remember that washing is very hard work; more young women break down their strength with washing than with any other toil. If young women would only remember not to mix together other work with washing; if they would not hurry too much to be smart about getting done; if they would lighten the task by soaking the clothes, and by using a clothes-wringer . . . instead of straining their chests and ruining their backs by lifting tubs of water, or boilers of clothes, or by carrying to the line a basket heaped with wet clothes . . . we should have fewer broken-down women.

Pioneers in the Western frontier used more primitive methods of washing. They rubbed and beat clothing with rocks in a river, and sometimes they had to substitute animal fat for the processed lye soaps of the East. No wonder that by the end of the 1800s many wealthy Americans hired a full-time servant just to do laundry!

These little girls, like little girls today, were playing house, imitating the housework they saw their mother doing, including washing the clothes using a tub and washboard.

Part II: Cooking, Cleaning, and Keeping House

EXTRA! EXTRA!

Chicago Daily Express
The Modern Woman

Beware, men! The modern woman not only wants to vote, smoke cigarettes, and wear trousers—she also wants freedom from the housework that has been woman's lot for countless centuries. "If my husband had to wash the laundry every single Monday of his life," proclaimed one woman in this writer's hearing, "he would have found some invention to do the work for him long ago." We suspect, however, that few men's work is hardly luxurious, nor is the responsibility of caring for his wife and family a light weight for any man to bear on his shoulders. We can only hope that women will find it in their hearts to continue to do their share around the home. It will be a sad world indeed if all the doctors, lawyers, and business men are forced to stay home on Mondays to do the laundry!

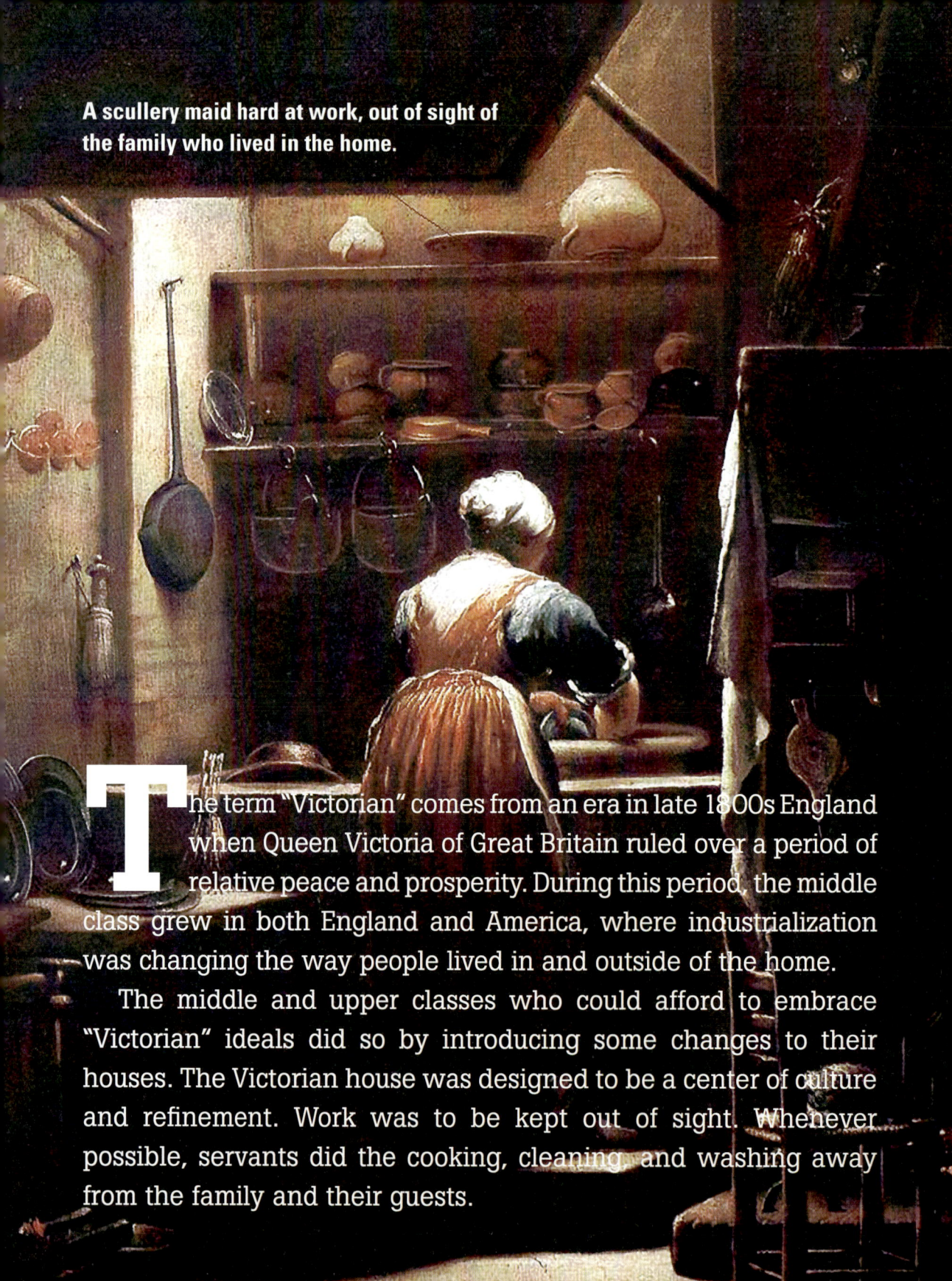

A scullery maid hard at work, out of sight of the family who lived in the home.

The term "Victorian" comes from an era in late 1800s England when Queen Victoria of Great Britain ruled over a period of relative peace and prosperity. During this period, the middle class grew in both England and America, where industrialization was changing the way people lived in and outside of the home.

The middle and upper classes who could afford to embrace "Victorian" ideals did so by introducing some changes to their houses. The Victorian house was designed to be a center of culture and refinement. Work was to be kept out of sight. Whenever possible, servants did the cooking, cleaning, and washing away from the family and their guests.

The Scullery

The scullery was the Victorian solution to keeping housework out of sight. Usually built near the back of the house, behind the kitchen, the scullery was where laundry and other cleaning was done. It was kept near the back of the house so that dirty water and other waste could be thrown out the back door. If a house could afford it, the scullery was outfitted with many of the laundry devices of the day. A copper bowl sat atop a fire for boiling linens. A "mangle" was used to push wet clothes through weighted wooden rollers to remove excess water.

A mangle, used for squeezing the water from laundered clothes.

A nineteenth-century "washing machine" and a trough for laying down the wet clothes.

A typical Victorian parlor.

The Parlor

The parlor was the one room that really represented the changes in a Victorian house. Usually situated somewhere near the front of the house, the parlor was used as a formal sitting room for entertaining guests. It was often closed during the week and opened only on weekends. The word parlor comes from the French word parler, which means "to speak," but the parlor was used for much more than just talking. It usually contained a family's best furniture, works of art, and other proud possessions.

The parlor would have a card table for games, a piano for entertaining guests, various paintings on the wall, and a fireplace for keeping everyone warm, usually with an ornate mantel around it and a mirror above it. Parlor pastimes included card games such as euchre, bridge, seven-up, and board games such as dominoes, checkers, and chess. Young ladies and their mothers might sit in the parlor to practice their needlework or to read a novel. In the late 1800s, thousands of pianos were sold to middle- and upper-class families, and they usually found their place in the parlor. Men, women, children, and guests would gather around a piano to sing or listen to one of the family members perform (usually a daughter).

Also, photography was becoming very popular in America at this time, and the parlor was often just the place for a family photograph.

Today, the parlor has become what we know as the living room. Couches or sofas replaced fancy chairs, and televisions replaced pianos, artwork, and card-tables.

The women of the family enjoyed "genteel" pastimes in the parlor.

The Bedroom

Most middle-class homes had very few bedrooms: one for the wife and husband, and another one for all the children. It was common to put two beds in a child's room, and to have more than one child sleep in a bed. Beds in lower-class homes were usually made of wood, but the upper classes preferred metal, brass, and iron, since these materials were less likely to provide hiding places for insects. Mattresses were made of feathers, if possible. Although feather bedding was expensive, a good night's sleep was highly valued, and many Americans considered the bed a symbol of a family's future happiness.

A typical children's bedroom in the 1800s.

52   Home Sweet Home: Around the House in the 1800s

In general, the bedroom was a dreary room. It was considered the most private place in a house. No one but family members entered, and so it was rarely decorated or well-lit. Usually, a jug and bowl were placed in the room for people to wash their hands and faces before bed. Wardrobes were used instead of closets, which didn't exist at the time.

No one in the 1800s needed a closet, since most middle-class Americans at that time had no more than three outfits! Because laundry was such a chore, clothes were rarely washed and usually made of tough materials in dull colors that hid dirt. Underwear included corsets and underskirts called petticoats for women, and woolen long-john underwear for men. Corsets were tightly laced tops that pinched the waist and pushed up the breasts. They were usually painful and sometimes even a health risk, as they could make breathing difficult. Beauty standards for women in that time made most clothing uncomfortable. Men of privilege had less to worry about—their standard of dress was a three-piece suit.

EXTRA! EXTRA!

Ferris Good Sense Corset Waist

Faultless form, delightful comfort, perfect health and grace—every breath a free one, every move an easy one—the invariable result of living in the Ferris Good Sense Corset Waist. The favorite of all women who wish to dress and feel well. Made in styles to suit every figure—long or short waist, high or low bust.

Affordable for every family, children's corset waists cost from 25 cents to 50 cents, misses' from 50 cents to 1 dollar, and ladies' from one dollar to two dollars. For sale by all retailers in the New York Area.

The Bathroom

In the 1800s, just to have a bathroom in one's house was a privilege. Bathrooms were for taking baths, not for using the toilet, which wouldn't arrive until indoor plumbing in the next century. Hygiene was difficult for Americans, who didn't fully understand the health benefits, and didn't have access to indoor plumbing. Even so, many wealthy families began to recognize the benefits of a daily bath.

All bathtubs were free standing, not built into walls as they are today. Tubs had to be filled with hot water heated on the stove and carried upstairs. Since heating the huge quantities of water required to fill a tub took a long time, the same water was used for every member of the family. By the fourth or fifth bath, it was usually cold and filthy. Soap was made of animal fat and vegetable oils. Some truly strange things were used as shampoos, including cow fat and perfume or eggs and lemons.

As gross as it may seem today, a bath in cold water with vegetable oil for soap was better than nothing. Those who couldn't afford a tub bathed even more infrequently. They smelled bad and were more likely to get sick. As the English novelist Somerset Maugham wrote, the morning bath "divides the classes more effectively than birth, wealth or education."

Bathrooms had other purposes besides bathing. For one, medicine

THE ORDER OF THE BATH

Pear's was one of the first commercially made soaps in the United States.

cabinets became popular in the 1800s and were often kept in bathrooms. Medicine cabinets contained many drugs, including narcotics that are illegal by today's standards, such as cocaine, opium, and heroin. Medical knowledge was still limited and the addictive quality of these drugs wasn't fully understood. Americans used powerful powders and elixirs to numb pain while the body attempted to heal itself.

If you were a woman who worried that you weren't fashionably plump, you might have kept this in your medicine cabinet!

Part III: The Victorian House

The Toilet

The toilet as we know it today didn't exist in the 1800s. In fact, doing one's business inside the house was still a relatively new idea! For centuries, the outhouse remained the only option for Americans. An outhouse was basically a wooden structure built atop a hole in the ground. Despite many attempts to make them more comfortable—different-sized holes for adults and children, padded seats—at the end of the day, the

An outhouse was a small building set back from the main house. Going out to do "your duty" could be a cold, lonely business.

Corn cobs were often used instead of toilet paper during the 1800s.

design remained the same. One can imagine the discomforts. Outhouses were cold, and often built far from the house to keep unwanted smells away.

The 1800s was a time of experimentation with new ideas for indoor toilets. The wealthy had access to some of the earlier experiments, such as the "earth closet." The earth closet would look to us like a small set of cabinets with a hole built into the top. It was built without access to indoor plumbing, with the idea that the person using it would heap a small shovel-full of dirt onto the waste.

Part III: The Victorian House 57

Almost every Victorian home of the late 1800s had a "chamber pot" in each bedroom. The chamber pot was usually stored beneath the bed, and removed and emptied by servants. The chamber pot existed since the Middle Ages, and it remained in use even with the invention of other indoor toilets. For Americans in the late 1800s, the chamber pot was an easy means of relieving oneself before bed, during the night, or first thing in morning.

The indoor water toilet had many names that persist today—the "water closet," the "privy," and others. The idea of flushing one's waste away with water was actually an old one, but it wasn't until the Victorian era that it became widely available. Both English and American inventors raced to invent the most efficient, pleasant toilet possible. By the late 1800s, people began to understand how disease was linked to waste. The old system of simply tossing chamber pots out open windows and into backyards was coming to an end. City planners wanted to develop a centralized sewer system that would allow city-dwellers to get rid of waste in a sanitary way.

A version of the "earth closet" developed in the 1880s.

On a cold winter night, a chamber pot like this was a good alternative to making a trip to the outhouse. In the morning, it would be emptied and cleaned for the following night.

EYEWITNESS ACCOUNT

The following is from a poem written as an ode to the outhouse, called "The Passing of the Outhouse" by James Whitcomb Riley:

When summer bloom began to fade
And winter to carouse,
We banked the little building
With a heap of hemlock boughs.
But when the crust was on the snow
And the sullen skies were gray,
In sooth the building was no place
Where one could wish to stay.
We did our duties promptly;
There one purpose swayed the mind.
We tarried not nor lingered long
On what we left behind.
The torture of that icy seat
Would made a Spartan sob,
For needs must scrape the gooseflesh
With a lacerating cob.
That from a frost-encrusted nail
Was suspended by a string —
My father was a frugal man
And wasted not a thing.
When grandpa had to "go out back"
And make his morning call,
We'd bundled up the dear old man
With a muffler and a shawl.
I knew the hole on which he sat
'Twas padded all around,
And once I dared to sit there;
'Twas all too wide, I found.
My loins were all too little
And I jack-knifed there to stay;
They had to come and get me out
Or I'd have passed away.

Part III: The Victorian House

In the early 1800s, John Howard Payne wrote a poem, which was set to music as a song that expressed the way Americans felt about their homes. During the dark days of the Civil War, when men were forced to leave their homes behind, the song was sung around both Northern and Southern campfires. President Lincoln and his wife claimed it as one of their favorite songs. Women embroidered its words on samplers and hung them in their parlors.

Today, its words are still familiar to us. Our homes have changed somewhat since the nineteenth century, but we still agree with the song's sentiments—there's just no place like home!

'Mid pleasures and palaces though we may roam,
Be it ever so humble, there's no place like home;
A charm from the sky seems to hallow us there,
Which, seek through the world, is ne'er met with elsewhere.
Home, home, sweet, sweet home!
There's no place like home, oh, there's no place like home!

Think About It

In *Home Sweet Home*, you've read about the major changes that occurred in the way people thought about their homes, and the way they lived in them, during the 1800s. One of the most significant changes was the evolution of the home from being a center of production—where all of the family worked within the home and its surrounding property to produce the things necessary to their daily lives, including food, clothing and either crops or merchandise to sell for income—to something closer to our modern understanding of "home" as a place separate from, even the opposite of, the workplace. The middle-class home of the later 1800s became a place of quiet, relaxation, comfort, and privacy where the man of the house went out to work while his wife (with the assistance of paid servants) cared for the home, prepared the meals, and raised the children. The parlor, with its fireside and piano, was the center, the heart, of the home. While these standards of comfort and economic security were not attainable by many, maybe most, Americans of the time, they remained the ideal for everyone, a major part of the "American Dream" for which millions were striving. These values remain with us today, despite the many economic and social changes that separate us from life in 1800s America.

- Home life in the 1800s was based on very defined and separate roles for men and women and boys and girls. What are some of the differences in household roles between then and now? Do you think people were happier in their home and family roles in the 1800s, or are they happier now?

- What do you think are some of the differences in family life between having a piano in the parlor to having a TV/DVD/Xbox in the living room as the "entertainment center" of the home?

- What do you think houses and family life will be like when you're an adult? What are some of the technological and social changes that will affect any changes between then and now?

Words Used in This Book

blacksmith: A craftsman who works in metal.

cobbler: An old name for someone who makes and repairs shoes.

domesticity: A devotion to home and family life.

efficient: Something that works well with a minimum of expense or effort

elixirs: Liquid mixtures, of varying medical value, which are believed to promote good health.

entrepreneurs: People who are motivated to build businesses and make money.

genre: A certain style or type of art or literature.

hygiene: The practice of cleanliness for health reasons.

ideal: The idea of something at its very best that is shared by members of a community.

Industrial Revolution: The period from around 1780 through the 1800s when rapid improvements in technology, agriculture, and manufacturing had a major effect on people's lives.

lacerating: Cutting, ripping, and tearing.

refinement: Having good manners, good taste, and an elegant lifestyle.

submissiveness: Unquestioning obedience to those in authority over you.

tanner: A person who processes animal hides into leather.

transition: A process of change over time.

Find Out More

In Books

Heidler, David S., Jeanne T. *Daily Life in the Early American Republic, 1790-1820: Creating a New Nation.* Westport, Conn.: Greenwood Press, 2004.

Moss, Randy. *Life in the Past: Victorian Homes.* Portsmouth, N.H.: Heinemann Library, 2004.

Muthesius, Stefan. *The Poetic Home: Designing the Nineteenth-Century Domestic Interior.* London, U.K.: Thames & Hudson, 2007.

Volo, James M., and Dorothy D. *Family Life in 19th-Century America.* Westport, Conn.: Greenwood Press, 2007.

Wilson, Laura. *Daily Life in a Victorian House.* London, U.K.: Puffin Books, 1999.

On the Internet

American Women and their Homes in the 1800s
xroads.virginia.edu/~MA02/rodriguez/GildedAge/home.html

Daily Life in the Victorian Era
www.erasofelegance.com/history/victorianlife.html

Domestic Servants in the 1800s
www.erasofelegance.com/history/victorianlife.html

Home Sweet Home: Life in 19th-century Ohio
lcweb2.loc.gov/diglib/ihas/html/ohio/ohio-home.html

The Industrial Revolution
www.teacheroz.com/19thcent.htm#industrial

The websites listed on this page were active at the time of publication. The publisher is not responsible for websites that have changed their address or discontinued operation since the date of publication. The publisher will review and update the websites upon each reprint.

Index

Balloon frame 26–27
bathroom 54–55
bedroom 28, 52–53, 57
Beecher, Catharine 42

Civil War 10, 28, 41, 59
cooking 18–19, 24, 29, 34–38, 40–41, 48
corsets 53

Europe 26, 36,

farms 16, 18–19, 22, 34,
fireplaces 31–32, 40–42, 51

Homestead Act 32

immigrants 24
Industrial Revolution 16, 24

larder 36–37
laundry 25, 44–46, 49, 53
log cabins 31–32

Native Americans 28–29, 37, 40
North 36, 41, 59
outhouse 56–58

parlor 50–51, 59
pioneers 31, 45

scullery 48–49
servants 22–25, 34, 38, 44–45, 48, 57
slaves 28
sod houses 30–32
South 28, 36–38, 59
stoves 32, 40–42, 54

toilets 54, 56–57

Victorian 48–51, 57

water 38–39, 44–45, 49, 54, 57
West 31–32, 38, 45
Wilder, Laura Ingalls 18
wood 26–27, 40–41, 52, 56

Picture Credits

Andrushko, Galyna; Fotolia: p. 40
Barskaya, Galina; Fotolia: p. 47
Bellows, George: p. 15
Cassatt, Mary: p. 24
Connor Prairie Living History Museum, Fishers, Indiana: p. 32
Creative Commons: pp. 16, 26, 27, 28, 29, 33, 36, 37, 48, 49, 56, 57, 58
Currier and Ives: pp. 8–9, 14–15, 59
Dover: pp. 22, 23
Johnson, Jonathan Eastman: pp. 14–15
Library of Congress: p. 25, 29, 44, 45, 46
Marquette, Bonnie C.; Fotolia: p. 28
Museum of Appalachia, courtesy of Carmen Bonnell: p. 17
New Jersey National Trust: p. 49
Ng, Joe; Dreamstime: p. 52
Saratoga Historical Museum: p. 37
Slate Run Living Historical Farm, Canal Winchester, Ohio: pp. 18, 19, 41
Steidl, James; Fotolia: p. 41
Washington County Historical Society of Ohio: p. 51
White Pine Village, Creative Commons: pp. 34–35

To the best knowledge of the publisher, all images not specifically credited are in the public domain. If any image has been inadvertently uncredited, please notify Harding House Publishing Service, 220 Front Street, Vestal, New York 13850, so that credit can be given in future printings.

About the Author and the Consultant

Zachary Chastain is an independent writer and actor living in Binghamton, New York. He is the author of various educational books for both younger and older audiences.

John Gillis is a Rutgers University Professor of History Emeritus. A graduate of Amherst College and Stanford University, he has taught at Stanford, Princeton, University of California at Berkeley, as well as Rutgers. Gillis is well known for his work in social history, including pioneering studies of age relations, marriage, and family. The author or editor of ten books, he has also been a fellow at both St. Antony's College, Oxford, and Clare Hall, Cambridge.